# Down

**Tony Bradman**
**Illustrated by Jon Stuart**

**OXFORD**

# The story so far ...

In the book *A Wild Ride* Max, Cat, Ant and Tiger make a micro-raft.

They go on a wild water ride through the park.

Then ... LOOK OUT!
Max, Cat and Tiger
jump from the
raft just in time.

The raft breaks but Ant holds on. He skims
across the water. He lands on the small island
in the middle of the pond.

Now Max, Cat and Tiger have to get him back ...

Max, Cat and Tiger looked across to the island. Ant had been there waving to them. Now he was gone.

Just then, a huge fish poked its head out of the pond. Its beady eye glared at the children. It opened its big mouth. Then it dropped back into the water and was gone.

"Oh, no!" cried Cat. "Maybe that horrible fish has caught Ant."

She checked her watch. A tiny green dot moved around. That showed Ant was OK … for now.

"Come on, Max," said Tiger. "We need a plan – and fast!"

Just then they heard a flapping noise. A shadow went over them. It gave Max an idea. "I know," said Max. "We can use the micro-copter to rescue Ant by air!"

"How will you get it?" said Cat. "Now it's stopped raining, there are lots of people about. You can't grow. It will take you ages to get back to the den."

"I'll think of something," said Max.

Max ran off into the grass beside the path. He was hidden there but the ground was wet. His feet got stuck in the mud. Huge drops of water fell on him. A dog splashed past.

"A dog …" thought Max.

Fast as a flea, Max jumped out of the wet grass. He took a ride on the passing dog.

"Thanks!" Max whispered when they got to the micro-den.

Max ran into the den. He went up to the bird box where he kept the micro-copter. Soon he was strapped in and ready to take off. He pressed the start button and rose into the air.

The rain had stopped but it was windy. It was hard to steer the micro-copter. He nearly crashed into a bush. "Whoops!" said Max. An angry bee flew at him.

Max dipped the micro-copter and flew up over the pond.

Cat and Tiger waved from down below.
"Be careful, Max!" Cat yelled.

Max was too busy to wave back. The pond
looked as wide as the ocean. The island
seemed far away.

He dipped the micro-copter down. Insects skimmed across the water. Then Max saw a huge shadow in the water below. He gulped. The big fish was there, watching and waiting ...

"Ant, where are you?" Max called out when he landed.

There was no answer. Max saw footprints in the mud so he followed them. He felt as if he was in a jungle. Birds sang and grasses rustled around him.

Ant, of course, was fine. In fact, he was having a great time.

"Oh, hi Max," he said when Max found him. "Look at this frogspawn. It's amazing."

"I'm here to rescue you, Ant," said Max.

"I don't want to be rescued," said Ant. "I'm having fun!"

Ant loved the island. There were lots of bugs and mini-beasts on it. His pockets were full with things he had collected.

"Come on," said Max. "You can't stay here.
I've got the micro-copter to fly you back."
Ant didn't like the idea but he agreed to go.

Max strapped himself and Ant in to the micro-copter. He pushed the starter button. *WHIRRR ... WHIRRR ...WHIRRR ...* went the copter. But it didn't lift them off the ground.

"It's no good," said Max. "We're too heavy.
You'll have to take all that stuff out of
your pockets."

"What?" squeaked Ant. "It's not stuff.
These are scientific samples …"

Max gave Ant a look.

"Oh, all right," grumbled Ant.

Max pressed the starter button. This time they rose into the air.

It had started to rain again. Large drops of water splashed down on the micro-copter. It was hard for Max to steer. As Max and Ant got wet, they got heavier.

The micro-copter flew lower and lower. It skimmed low over the water. The shadow of the big fish moved beneath them.

"Don't look down, Ant!" said Max.

"I won't ..." said Ant.

Just then, there was a loud *PLOP!* Then another ... and another.

"Look!" cried Max." It's Cat and Tiger to the rescue!"

Cat and Tiger were throwing pebbles into the pond. They scared the fish away … just in time. The micro-copter spluttered and spun to the ground. Max and Ant got out. They were shaken but safe.

"Tomorrow, I vote that we do something boring!" said Max.

# Tell the story ...

**1**

**2**

**3**

**4**

**5**

**6**